THIS CRUISE JOURNAL BELONGS TO:

_____

CRUISE SAVINGS

WE'RE SAVING FOR: _____

AMOUNT NEEDED: _____

OUR GOAL DATE: _____

$

DEPOSIT TRACKER

AMOUNT DEPOSITED:	DATE DEPOSITED:
$	
$	
$	
$	
$	
$	
$	
$	
$	
$	

CRUISE SAVINGS

DEPOSIT TRACKER

AMOUNT DEPOSITED: **DATE DEPOSITED:**

$ _____ _____

$ _____ _____

$ _____ _____

$ _____ _____

$ _____ _____

$ _____ _____

$ _____ _____

$ _____ _____

$ _____ _____

$ _____ _____

$ _____ _____

$ _____ _____

$ _____ _____

CRUISE DETAILS

NOTES

TO DO:

CRUISE DETAILS & REMINDERS:

FLIGHT INFORMATION

DATE: _____ DESTINATION: _____

AIRLINE:	
BOOKING NUMBER:	
DEPARTURE DATE:	
BOARDING TIME:	
GATE NUMBER:	
SEAT NUMBER:	
ARRIVAL / LANDING TIME:	

DATE: _____ DESTINATION: _____

AIRLINE:	
BOOKING NUMBER:	
DEPARTURE DATE:	
BOARDING TIME:	
GATE NUMBER:	
SEAT NUMBER:	
ARRIVAL / LANDING TIME:	

FLIGHT INFORMATION

DATE: _____ DESTINATION: _____

AIRLINE:	
BOOKING NUMBER:	
DEPARTURE DATE:	
BOARDING TIME:	
GATE NUMBER:	
SEAT NUMBER:	
ARRIVAL / LANDING TIME:	

DATE: _____ DESTINATION: _____

AIRLINE:	
BOOKING NUMBER:	
DEPARTURE DATE:	
BOARDING TIME:	
GATE NUMBER:	
SEAT NUMBER:	
ARRIVAL / LANDING TIME:	

TRAIN INFORMATION

DATE: _____ DESTINATION: _____

DEPARTING STATION:	
TICKET TYPE:	
DEPARTURE DATE:	
BOARDING TIME:	
GATE NUMBER:	
SEAT NUMBER:	
ARRIVAL / LANDING TIME:	

DATE: _____ DESTINATION: _____

AIRLINE:	
BOOKING NUMBER:	
DEPARTURE DATE:	
BOARDING TIME:	
GATE NUMBER:	
SEAT NUMBER:	
ARRIVAL / LANDING TIME:	

CAR INFORMATION

DATE: _____ PICK-UP LOCATION: _____

CAR RENTAL COMPANY:	
VEHICLE TYPE:	
DEPARTURE DATE:	
PICK-UP TIME:	
INSPECTION NOTES:	
COST PER DAY:	
RETURN DATE:	

DATE: _____ PICK-UP LOCATION:: _____

CAR RENTAL COMPANY:	
VEHICLE TYPE:	
DEPARTURE DATE:	
PICK-UP TIME:	
INSPECTION NOTES:	
COST PER DAY:	
RETURN DATE:	

CRUISE COUNTDOWN

MONTH: _____   YEAR: _____

M	T	W	T	F	S	S

PACKING LIST IDEAS

CLOTHING FOR HER	✓	CLOTHING FOR HIM	✓
T-Shirts &, Tank Tops & Blouses		T-Shirts & Tank Tops	
Sundresses		Shorts	
Flip Flops, Sandals & Heels		Swim Wear	
Shorts & Pants		Jeans, Khakis	
Swimsuit & Cover Up		Formal Attire (dress shirt, shoes, etc.)	
Purses		Belt	
Aqua/Swimming Shoes		Tie	
Bras, Panties & Socks		Sandals / Sneakers	
Sunhat		Visor, Baseball Cap	
Sunglasses		Watch	
Formal Attire		Sunglasses	
Jewelry		Socks & Underwear	

ESSENTIALS	✓	FOR THE JOURNEY	✓
Sporting Goods		Carry On Bag	
Suntan Lotion		Cash / Local Currency	
Medication (motion sickness, etc.)		Credit Cards	
Travel Mug / Water Bottle		Phone Charger	
Games		Backpack	
Jacket		IMPORTANT DOCUMENTS	✓
Toiletries		Passport & ID	
Hiking Boots		Cruise Documents & Boarding Pass	
		Flight Information	

PACKING CHECKLIST

CLOTHING FOR HER	✓	CLOTHING FOR HIM	✓

ESSENTIALS	✓	FOR THE JOURNEY	✓
		IMPORTANT DOCUMENTS	✓

CRUISE PACKING CHECKLIST

CLOTHING	✓	ESSENTIALS	✓

CRUISE EXCURSION PLANNER

ACTIVITY / EXCURSION OVERVIEW:

EST COST OF EXCURSION: _____

INCLUSIONS: ✓

- FOOD & DRINK: ☐
- TRANSPORTATION: ☐
- GRATUITY: ☐

EXCLUSIONS: ✓

- _____ ☐
- _____ ☐
- _____ ☐

ACTUAL COST: [   ]

IMPORTANT INFORMATION:

CONTACT: _____   PHONE #: _____

MEET UP TIME: _____   WHAT TO BRING: _____

ADDRESS: _____

CRUISE EXCURSION PLANNER

ACTIVITY / EXCURSION OVERVIEW:

EST COST OF EXCURSION: _____

INCLUSIONS: ✓	**EXCLUSIONS:** ✓
FOOD & DRINK: ☐	_____ ☐
TRANSPORTATION: ☐	_____ ☐
GRATUITY: ☐	_____ ☐

ACTUAL COST: [ ]

IMPORTANT INFORMATION:

CONTACT: _____   PHONE #: _____

MEET UP TIME: _____   WHAT TO BRING: _____

ADDRESS: _____

CRUISE EXCURSION PLANNER

ACTIVITY / EXCURSION OVERVIEW:

EST COST OF EXCURSION: _____

INCLUSIONS: ✓	**EXCLUSIONS:** ✓
FOOD & DRINK: ☐	_____ ☐
TRANSPORTATION: ☐	_____ ☐
GRATUITY: ☐	_____ ☐

ACTUAL COST: _____

IMPORTANT INFORMATION:

CONTACT: _____ PHONE #: _____

MEET UP TIME: _____ WHAT TO BRING: _____

ADDRESS: _____

CRUISE EXCURSION PLANNER

ACTIVITY / EXCURSION OVERVIEW:

EST COST OF EXCURSION: _____

INCLUSIONS: ✓	**EXCLUSIONS:** ✓
FOOD & DRINK: ☐	_____ ☐
TRANSPORTATION: ☐	_____ ☐
GRATUITY: ☐	_____ ☐

ACTUAL COST: [ ]

IMPORTANT INFORMATION:

CONTACT: _____   PHONE #: _____

MEET UP TIME: _____   WHAT TO BRING: _____

ADDRESS: _____

CRUISE PORT PLANNER

DESTINATION: DATE:

THINGS TO DO / SEE:

- [ ]
- [ ]
- [ ]
- [ ]
- [ ]
- [ ]
- [ ]

WHERE TO EAT:

- [ ]
- [ ]
- [ ]
- [ ]
- [ ]
- [ ]
- [ ]

TRANSPORTATION DETAILS:

- [ ]
- [ ]
- [ ]
- [ ]
- [ ]

OTHER INFORMATION:

- [ ]
- [ ]
- [ ]
- [ ]
- [ ]

RETURN TO SHIP BY:

CRUISE PORT PLANNER

DESTINATION: **DATE:**

THINGS TO DO / SEE:

- [ ]
- [ ]
- [ ]
- [ ]
- [ ]
- [ ]
- [ ]

WHERE TO EAT:

- [ ]
- [ ]
- [ ]
- [ ]
- [ ]
- [ ]
- [ ]

TRANSPORTATION DETAILS:

- [ ]
- [ ]
- [ ]
- [ ]
- [ ]

OTHER INFORMATION:

- [ ]
- [ ]
- [ ]
- [ ]
- [ ]

RETURN TO SHIP BY:

CRUISE PORT PLANNER

DESTINATION: **DATE:**

THINGS TO DO / SEE:

- [ ]
- [ ]
- [ ]
- [ ]
- [ ]
- [ ]
- [ ]

WHERE TO EAT:

- [ ]
- [ ]
- [ ]
- [ ]
- [ ]
- [ ]
- [ ]

TRANSPORTATION DETAILS:

- [ ]
- [ ]
- [ ]
- [ ]
- [ ]

OTHER INFORMATION:

- [ ]
- [ ]
- [ ]
- [ ]
- [ ]

RETURN TO SHIP BY:

CRUISE PORT PLANNER

DESTINATION: DATE:

THINGS TO DO / SEE:

WHERE TO EAT:

TRANSPORTATION DETAILS:

OTHER INFORMATION:

RETURN TO SHIP BY:

CRUISE PORT PLANNER

DESTINATION: **DATE:**

THINGS TO DO / SEE:

- [ ]
- [ ]
- [ ]
- [ ]
- [ ]
- [ ]
- [ ]

WHERE TO EAT:

- [ ]
- [ ]
- [ ]
- [ ]
- [ ]
- [ ]
- [ ]

TRANSPORTATION DETAILS:

- [ ]
- [ ]
- [ ]
- [ ]
- [ ]

OTHER INFORMATION:

- [ ]
- [ ]
- [ ]
- [ ]
- [ ]

RETURN TO SHIP BY:

CRUISE PORT PLANNER

DESTINATION: **DATE:**

THINGS TO DO / SEE:

WHERE TO EAT:

TRANSPORTATION DETAILS:

OTHER INFORMATION:

RETURN TO SHIP BY:

CRUISE PORT PLANNER

DESTINATION: **DATE:**

THINGS TO DO / SEE:

WHERE TO EAT:

TRANSPORTATION DETAILS:

OTHER INFORMATION:

RETURN TO SHIP BY:

CRUISE PORT PLANNER

DESTINATION: DATE:

THINGS TO DO / SEE:

WHERE TO EAT:

TRANSPORTATION DETAILS:

OTHER INFORMATION:

RETURN TO SHIP BY:

CRUISE PORT PLANNER

DESTINATION: DATE:

THINGS TO DO / SEE:

WHERE TO EAT:

TRANSPORTATION DETAILS:

OTHER INFORMATION:

RETURN TO SHIP BY:

CRUISE PORT PLANNER

DESTINATION: DATE:

THINGS TO DO / SEE:

WHERE TO EAT:

TRANSPORTATION DETAILS:

OTHER INFORMATION:

RETURN TO SHIP BY:

CRUISE PORT PLANNER

DESTINATION: DATE:

THINGS TO DO / SEE:

WHERE TO EAT:

TRANSPORTATION DETAILS:

OTHER INFORMATION:

RETURN TO SHIP BY:

CRUISE PORT PLANNER

DESTINATION: **DATE:**

THINGS TO DO / SEE:

WHERE TO EAT:

TRANSPORTATION DETAILS:

OTHER INFORMATION:

RETURN TO SHIP BY:

CRUISE PORT PLANNER

DESTINATION: DATE:

THINGS TO DO / SEE:

WHERE TO EAT:

TRANSPORTATION DETAILS:

OTHER INFORMATION:

RETURN TO SHIP BY:

CRUISE PORT PLANNER

DESTINATION: DATE:

THINGS TO DO / SEE:

WHERE TO EAT:

TRANSPORTATION DETAILS:

OTHER INFORMATION:

RETURN TO SHIP BY:

ALL ABOARD!

PRE-CRUISE TO DO LIST & CHECKLIST

1 MONTH BEFORE

- [ ]
- [ ]
- [ ]
- [ ]
- [ ]

2 WEEKS BEFORE

- [ ]
- [ ]
- [ ]
- [ ]
- [ ]

1 WEEK BEFORE

- [ ]
- [ ]
- [ ]
- [ ]
- [ ]

2 DAYS BEFORE

- [ ]
- [ ]
- [ ]
- [ ]
- [ ]

24 HOURS BEFORE

- [ ]
- [ ]
- [ ]
- [ ]
- [ ]

DAY OF TRAVEL

- [ ]
- [ ]
- [ ]
- [ ]
- [ ]

CRUISE PLANNER

WEEK OF:

MONDAY	TUESDAY	WEDNESDAY	THURSDAY
TO DO	TO DO	TO DO	TO DO
MEALS	MEALS	MEALS	MEALS

FRIDAY	SATURDAY	SUNDAY	NOTES
TO DO	TO DO	TO DO	
MEALS	MEALS	MEALS	MEALS

CRUISE PLANNER

WEEK OF:

MONDAY	TUESDAY	WEDNESDAY	THURSDAY
TO DO	TO DO	TO DO	TO DO
MEALS	MEALS	MEALS	MEALS

FRIDAY	SATURDAY	SUNDAY	NOTES
TO DO	TO DO	TO DO	
MEALS	MEALS	MEALS	MEALS

CRUISING TO DO LIST

CRUISE BUCKET LIST

PLACES I WANT TO VISIT:

THINGS I WANT TO SEE:

TOP 3 DESTINATIONS:

CRUISE ITINERARY

Monday

Tuesday

Wednesday

Thursday

Friday

Saturday

Sunday

CRUISE ITINERARY

Monday

Tuesday

Wednesday

Thursday

Friday

Saturday

Sunday

CRUISE ITINERARY

Monday

Tuesday

Wednesday

Thursday

Friday

Saturday

Sunday

CRUISE OVERVIEW

MONTH:

MONDAY	TUESDAY	WEDNESDAY	THURSDAY	FRIDAY	SATURDAY	SUNDAY

CRUISE ACTIVITIES

WEEKLY ACTIVITY TRACKER: **M T W T F S S**

DAILY ACTIVITY PLANNER

DAILY ITINERARY

ACTIVITY: _____

TIME: _____

LOCATION: _____

WEATHER:

MEAL PLANNER

DAILY EXPENSES

TOTAL COST: _____

TOP ACTIVITIES

TIME:	SCHEDULE:

NOTES:

DAILY ACTIVITY PLANNER

DAILY ITINERARY

ACTIVITY: _____

TIME: _____

LOCATION: _____

WEATHER: ☀️ 🌤️ 🌦️ ☁️ ⛈️

MEAL PLANNER

DAILY EXPENSES

TOTAL COST: [ ]

TOP ACTIVITIES

TIME:	SCHEDULE:

NOTES:

DAILY ACTIVITY PLANNER

DAILY ITINERARY

ACTIVITY: _____
TIME: _____
LOCATION: _____
WEATHER: ☀️ ⛅ 🌦️ ☁️ ⛈️

MEAL PLANNER

DAILY EXPENSES

_____ _____

_____ _____

_____ _____

_____ _____

TOTAL COST: [_____]

TOP ACTIVITIES

TIME:	SCHEDULE:

NOTES:

DAILY ACTIVITY PLANNER

DAILY ITINERARY

ACTIVITY: _____

TIME: _____

LOCATION: _____

WEATHER: ☀️ 🌤️ 🌦️ ☁️ ⛈️

MEAL PLANNER

DAILY EXPENSES

TOTAL COST: ☐

TOP ACTIVITIES

TIME: SCHEDULE:

NOTES:

DAILY ACTIVITY PLANNER

DAILY ITINERARY

ACTIVITY: _____

TIME: _____

LOCATION: _____

WEATHER: ☀ ⛅ 🌦 ☁ ⛈

MEAL PLANNER

DAILY EXPENSES

TOTAL COST: _____

TOP ACTIVITIES

TIME:	SCHEDULE:

NOTES:

DAILY ACTIVITY PLANNER

DAILY ITINERARY

ACTIVITY: _____

TIME: _____

LOCATION: _____

WEATHER: ☀️ 🌤️ 🌦️ ☁️ ⛈️

MEAL PLANNER

DAILY EXPENSES

TOTAL COST: [ ]

TOP ACTIVITIES

TIME:	SCHEDULE:

NOTES:

DAILY ACTIVITY PLANNER

DAILY ITINERARY

ACTIVITY: _____
TIME: _____
LOCATION: _____
WEATHER:

MEAL PLANNER

DAILY EXPENSES

TOTAL COST: _____

TOP ACTIVITIES

TIME:	SCHEDULE:

NOTES:

DAILY ACTIVITY PLANNER

DAILY ITINERARY

ACTIVITY: _____

TIME: _____

LOCATION: _____

WEATHER: ☀️ ⛅ 🌦️ ☁️ ⛈️

MEAL PLANNER

DAILY EXPENSES

TOTAL COST: [ ]

TOP ACTIVITIES

TIME:	SCHEDULE:

NOTES:

DAILY ACTIVITY PLANNER

DAILY ITINERARY

ACTIVITY: _____

TIME: _____

LOCATION: _____

WEATHER: ☀️ ⛅ 🌦️ ☁️ ⛈️

MEAL PLANNER

DAILY EXPENSES

_____   _____

_____   _____

_____   _____

_____   _____

TOTAL COST: [_____]

TOP ACTIVITIES

TIME:	SCHEDULE:

NOTES:

DAILY ACTIVITY PLANNER

DAILY ITINERARY

ACTIVITY: _____
TIME: _____
LOCATION: _____
WEATHER: ☀️ ⛅ 🌦️ ☁️ ⛈️

MEAL PLANNER

DAILY EXPENSES

TOTAL COST: [ ]

TOP ACTIVITIES

TIME:	SCHEDULE:

NOTES:

DAILY ACTIVITY PLANNER

DAILY ITINERARY

ACTIVITY: _____
TIME: _____
LOCATION: _____
WEATHER: ☀️ ⛅ 🌦️ ☁️ ⛈️

MEAL PLANNER

DAILY EXPENSES

_____   _____
_____   _____
_____   _____
_____   _____

TOTAL COST: [   ]

TOP ACTIVITIES

TIME:	SCHEDULE:

NOTES:

DAILY ACTIVITY PLANNER

DAILY ITINERARY

ACTIVITY: _____
TIME: _____
LOCATION: _____
WEATHER: ☀️ ⛅ 🌦️ ☁️ ⛈️

MEAL PLANNER

DAILY EXPENSES

TOTAL COST: ☐

TOP ACTIVITIES

TIME:	SCHEDULE:

NOTES:

CRUISE FRIENDS

FRIENDS ARE FOREVER

NAME:

PHONE NUMBER:

ADDRESS:

CABIN #:

FRIENDS ARE FOREVER

NAME:

PHONE NUMBER:

ADDRESS:

CABIN #:

FRIENDS ARE FOREVER

NAME:

PHONE NUMBER:

ADDRESS:

CABIN #:

FRIENDS ARE FOREVER

NAME:

PHONE NUMBER:

ADDRESS:

CABIN #:

There's Nothing Like Cruising Life!

CRUISE FRIENDS

FRIENDS ARE FOREVER

NAME:

PHONE NUMBER:

ADDRESS:

CABIN #:

FRIENDS ARE FOREVER

NAME:

PHONE NUMBER:

ADDRESS:

CABIN #:

FRIENDS ARE FOREVER

NAME:

PHONE NUMBER:

ADDRESS:

CABIN #:

FRIENDS ARE FOREVER

NAME:

PHONE NUMBER:

ADDRESS:

CABIN #:

There's Nothing Like Cruising Life!

CRUISE FRIENDS

FRIENDS ARE FOREVER

NAME:

PHONE NUMBER:

ADDRESS:

CABIN #:

FRIENDS ARE FOREVER

NAME:

PHONE NUMBER:

ADDRESS:

CABIN #:

FRIENDS ARE FOREVER

NAME:

PHONE NUMBER:

ADDRESS:

CABIN #:

FRIENDS ARE FOREVER

NAME:

PHONE NUMBER:

ADDRESS:

CABIN #:

There's Nothing Like Cruising Life!

CRUISE FRIENDS

FRIENDS ARE FOREVER

NAME:
PHONE NUMBER:
ADDRESS:
CABIN #:

FRIENDS ARE FOREVER

NAME:
PHONE NUMBER:
ADDRESS:
CABIN #:

FRIENDS ARE FOREVER

NAME:
PHONE NUMBER:
ADDRESS:
CABIN #:

FRIENDS ARE FOREVER

NAME:
PHONE NUMBER:
ADDRESS:
CABIN #:

There's Nothing Like Cruising Life!

MY CRUISE AGENDA

MY CRUISE JOURNAL

DATE:

What I Did Today:

Highlight of the Day:

Thoughts & Reflections:

MY CRUISE JOURNAL

DATE:

What I Did Today:

Highlight of the Day:

Thoughts & Reflections:

MY CRUISE JOURNAL

DATE:

What I Did Today:

Highlight of the Day:

Thoughts & Reflections:

MY CRUISE JOURNAL

DATE:

What I Did Today:

Highlight of the Day:

Thoughts & Reflections:

MY CRUISE JOURNAL

DATE:

What I Did Today:

Highlight of the Day:

Thoughts & Reflections:

MY CRUISE JOURNAL

DATE:

What I Did Today:

Highlight of the Day:

Thoughts & Reflections:

MY CRUISE JOURNAL

DATE:

What I Did Today:

Highlight of the Day:

Thoughts & Reflections:

MY CRUISE JOURNAL

DATE:

What I Did Today:

Highlight of the Day:

Thoughts & Reflections:

MY CRUISE JOURNAL

DATE:

What I Did Today:

Highlight of the Day:

Thoughts & Reflections:

MY CRUISE JOURNAL

DATE:

What I Did Today:

Highlight of the Day:

Thoughts & Reflections:

MY CRUISE JOURNAL

DATE:

What I Did Today:

Highlight of the Day:

Thoughts & Reflections:

MY CRUISE JOURNAL

DATE:

What I Did Today:

Highlight of the Day:

Thoughts & Reflections:

MY CRUISE JOURNAL

DATE:

What I Did Today:

Highlight of the Day:

Thoughts & Reflections:

MY CRUISE JOURNAL

DATE:

What I Did Today:

Highlight of the Day:

Thoughts & Reflections:

CRUISE SAVINGS

WE'RE SAVING FOR: _____

AMOUNT NEEDED: _____ $

OUR GOAL DATE: _____

DEPOSIT TRACKER

AMOUNT DEPOSITED:	DATE DEPOSITED:
$	
$	
$	
$	
$	
$	
$	
$	
$	
$	

CRUISE SAVINGS
DEPOSIT TRACKER

AMOUNT DEPOSITED: DATE DEPOSITED:

$
$
$
$
$
$
$
$
$
$
$
$
$
$

CRUISE DETAILS

NOTES

TO DO:

CRUISE DETAILS & REMINDERS:

FLIGHT INFORMATION

DATE: _____   DESTINATION: _____

AIRLINE:	
BOOKING NUMBER:	
DEPARTURE DATE:	
BOARDING TIME:	
GATE NUMBER:	
SEAT NUMBER:	
ARRIVAL / LANDING TIME:	

DATE: _____   DESTINATION: _____

AIRLINE:	
BOOKING NUMBER:	
DEPARTURE DATE:	
BOARDING TIME:	
GATE NUMBER:	
SEAT NUMBER:	
ARRIVAL / LANDING TIME:	

FLIGHT INFORMATION

DATE: _____ DESTINATION: _____

AIRLINE:	
BOOKING NUMBER:	
DEPARTURE DATE:	
BOARDING TIME:	
GATE NUMBER:	
SEAT NUMBER:	
ARRIVAL / LANDING TIME:	

DATE: _____ DESTINATION: _____

AIRLINE:	
BOOKING NUMBER:	
DEPARTURE DATE:	
BOARDING TIME:	
GATE NUMBER:	
SEAT NUMBER:	
ARRIVAL / LANDING TIME:	

TRAIN INFORMATION

DATE: _____ DESTINATION: _____

DEPARTING STATION:	
TICKET TYPE:	
DEPARTURE DATE:	
BOARDING TIME:	
GATE NUMBER:	
SEAT NUMBER:	
ARRIVAL / LANDING TIME:	

DATE: _____ DESTINATION: _____

AIRLINE:	
BOOKING NUMBER:	
DEPARTURE DATE:	
BOARDING TIME:	
GATE NUMBER:	
SEAT NUMBER:	
ARRIVAL / LANDING TIME:	

CAR INFORMATION

DATE: _____ PICK-UP LOCATION: _____

CAR RENTAL COMPANY:	
VEHICLE TYPE:	
DEPARTURE DATE:	
PICK-UP TIME:	
INSPECTION NOTES:	
COST PER DAY:	
RETURN DATE:	

DATE: _____ PICK-UP LOCATION:: _____

CAR RENTAL COMPANY:	
VEHICLE TYPE:	
DEPARTURE DATE:	
PICK-UP TIME:	
INSPECTION NOTES:	
COST PER DAY:	
RETURN DATE:	

CRUISE COUNTDOWN

MONTH: _____ YEAR: _____

M	T	W	T	F	S	S

PACKING LIST IDEAS

CLOTHING FOR HER	✓	CLOTHING FOR HIM	✓
T-Shirts &, Tank Tops & Blouses		T-Shirts & Tank Tops	
Sundresses		Shorts	
Flip Flops, Sandals & Heels		Swim Wear	
Shorts & Pants		Jeans, Khakis	
Swimsuit & Cover Up		Formal Attire (dress shirt, shoes, etc.)	
Purses		Belt	
Aqua/Swimming Shoes		Tie	
Bras, Panties & Socks		Sandals / Sneakers	
Sunhat		Visor, Baseball Cap	
Sunglasses		Watch	
Formal Attire		Sunglasses	
Jewelry		Socks & Underwear	

ESSENTIALS	✓	FOR THE JOURNEY	✓
Sporting Goods		Carry On Bag	
Suntan Lotion		Cash / Local Currency	
Medication (motion sickness, etc.)		Credit Cards	
Travel Mug / Water Bottle		Phone Charger	
Games		Backpack	
Jacket		IMPORTANT DOCUMENTS	✓
Toiletries		Passport & ID	
Hiking Boots		Cruise Documents & Boarding Pass	
		Flight Information	

PACKING CHECKLIST

CLOTHING FOR HER	✓	CLOTHING FOR HIM	✓

ESSENTIALS	✓	FOR THE JOURNEY	✓
		IMPORTANT DOCUMENTS	✓

CRUISE PACKING CHECKLIST

CLOTHING	✓	ESSENTIALS	✓

CRUISE EXCURSION PLANNER

ACTIVITY / EXCURSION OVERVIEW:

EST COST OF EXCURSION: _____

INCLUSIONS: ✓	**EXCLUSIONS:** ✓
FOOD & DRINK: ☐	_____ ☐
TRANSPORTATION: ☐	_____ ☐
GRATUITY: ☐	_____ ☐

ACTUAL COST: _____

IMPORTANT INFORMATION:

CONTACT: _____ PHONE #: _____

MEET UP TIME: _____ WHAT TO BRING: _____

ADDRESS: _____

CRUISE EXCURSION PLANNER

ACTIVITY / EXCURSION OVERVIEW:

EST COST OF EXCURSION: _____

INCLUSIONS: ✓	**EXCLUSIONS:** ✓
FOOD & DRINK: ☐	_____ ☐
TRANSPORTATION: ☐	_____ ☐
GRATUITY: ☐	_____ ☐

ACTUAL COST: _____

IMPORTANT INFORMATION:

CONTACT: _____ PHONE #: _____

MEET UP TIME: _____ WHAT TO BRING: _____

ADDRESS: _____

CRUISE EXCURSION PLANNER

ACTIVITY / EXCURSION OVERVIEW:

EST COST OF EXCURSION: _____

INCLUSIONS: ✓	**EXCLUSIONS:** ✓
FOOD & DRINK: ☐	_____ ☐
TRANSPORTATION: ☐	_____ ☐
GRATUITY: ☐	_____ ☐

ACTUAL COST: [   ]

IMPORTANT INFORMATION:

CONTACT: _____   PHONE #: _____

MEET UP TIME: _____   WHAT TO BRING: _____

ADDRESS: _____

CRUISE EXCURSION PLANNER

ACTIVITY / EXCURSION OVERVIEW:

EST COST OF EXCURSION: _____

INCLUSIONS: ✓	**EXCLUSIONS:** ✓
FOOD & DRINK: ☐	_____ ☐
TRANSPORTATION: ☐	_____ ☐
GRATUITY: ☐	_____ ☐

ACTUAL COST: _____

IMPORTANT INFORMATION:

CONTACT: _____ PHONE #: _____

MEET UP TIME: _____ WHAT TO BRING: _____

ADDRESS: _____

CRUISE PORT PLANNER

DESTINATION: DATE:

THINGS TO DO / SEE:

WHERE TO EAT:

TRANSPORTATION DETAILS:

OTHER INFORMATION:

RETURN TO SHIP BY:

CRUISE PORT PLANNER

DESTINATION: **DATE:**

THINGS TO DO / SEE:

WHERE TO EAT:

TRANSPORTATION DETAILS:

OTHER INFORMATION:

RETURN TO SHIP BY:

CRUISE PORT PLANNER

DESTINATION: DATE:

THINGS TO DO / SEE:

WHERE TO EAT:

TRANSPORTATION DETAILS:

OTHER INFORMATION:

RETURN TO SHIP BY:

CRUISE PORT PLANNER

DESTINATION: DATE:

THINGS TO DO / SEE:

WHERE TO EAT:

TRANSPORTATION DETAILS:

OTHER INFORMATION:

RETURN TO SHIP BY:

CRUISE PORT PLANNER

DESTINATION: _____   DATE: _____

THINGS TO DO / SEE:
- ☐
- ☐
- ☐
- ☐
- ☐
- ☐
- ☐

WHERE TO EAT:
- ☐
- ☐
- ☐
- ☐
- ☐
- ☐
- ☐

TRANSPORTATION DETAILS:
- ☐
- ☐
- ☐
- ☐
- ☐

OTHER INFORMATION:
- ☐
- ☐
- ☐
- ☐
- ☐

RETURN TO SHIP BY: _____

CRUISE PORT PLANNER

DESTINATION: **DATE:**

THINGS TO DO / SEE:

- [ ]
- [ ]
- [ ]
- [ ]
- [ ]
- [ ]
- [ ]

WHERE TO EAT:

- [ ]
- [ ]
- [ ]
- [ ]
- [ ]
- [ ]
- [ ]

TRANSPORTATION DETAILS:

- [ ]
- [ ]
- [ ]
- [ ]
- [ ]

OTHER INFORMATION:

- [ ]
- [ ]
- [ ]
- [ ]
- [ ]

RETURN TO SHIP BY:

CRUISE PORT PLANNER

DESTINATION: DATE:

THINGS TO DO / SEE:

WHERE TO EAT:

TRANSPORTATION DETAILS:

OTHER INFORMATION:

RETURN TO SHIP BY:

CRUISE PORT PLANNER

DESTINATION: DATE:

THINGS TO DO / SEE:

WHERE TO EAT:

TRANSPORTATION DETAILS:

OTHER INFORMATION:

RETURN TO SHIP BY:

CRUISE PORT PLANNER

DESTINATION: DATE:

THINGS TO DO / SEE:

WHERE TO EAT:

TRANSPORTATION DETAILS:

OTHER INFORMATION:

RETURN TO SHIP BY:

CRUISE PORT PLANNER

DESTINATION: **DATE:**

THINGS TO DO / SEE:

- [ ]
- [ ]
- [ ]
- [ ]
- [ ]
- [ ]
- [ ]

WHERE TO EAT:

- [ ]
- [ ]
- [ ]
- [ ]
- [ ]
- [ ]
- [ ]

TRANSPORTATION DETAILS:

- [ ]
- [ ]
- [ ]
- [ ]
- [ ]

OTHER INFORMATION:

- [ ]
- [ ]
- [ ]
- [ ]
- [ ]

RETURN TO SHIP BY:

CRUISE PORT PLANNER

DESTINATION: DATE:

THINGS TO DO / SEE:

WHERE TO EAT:

TRANSPORTATION DETAILS:

OTHER INFORMATION:

RETURN TO SHIP BY:

CRUISE PORT PLANNER

DESTINATION: DATE:

THINGS TO DO / SEE:

- [ ]
- [ ]
- [ ]
- [ ]
- [ ]
- [ ]
- [ ]

WHERE TO EAT:

- [ ]
- [ ]
- [ ]
- [ ]
- [ ]
- [ ]
- [ ]

TRANSPORTATION DETAILS:

- [ ]
- [ ]
- [ ]
- [ ]
- [ ]

OTHER INFORMATION:

- [ ]
- [ ]
- [ ]
- [ ]
- [ ]

RETURN TO SHIP BY:

CRUISE PORT PLANNER

DESTINATION: DATE:

THINGS TO DO / SEE:

- [ ]
- [ ]
- [ ]
- [ ]
- [ ]
- [ ]
- [ ]

WHERE TO EAT:

- [ ]
- [ ]
- [ ]
- [ ]
- [ ]
- [ ]
- [ ]

TRANSPORTATION DETAILS:

- [ ]
- [ ]
- [ ]
- [ ]
- [ ]

OTHER INFORMATION:

- [ ]
- [ ]
- [ ]
- [ ]
- [ ]

RETURN TO SHIP BY:

CRUISE PORT PLANNER

DESTINATION: **DATE:**

THINGS TO DO / SEE:

- [ ]
- [ ]
- [ ]
- [ ]
- [ ]
- [ ]
- [ ]

WHERE TO EAT:

- [ ]
- [ ]
- [ ]
- [ ]
- [ ]
- [ ]
- [ ]

TRANSPORTATION DETAILS:

- [ ]
- [ ]
- [ ]
- [ ]
- [ ]

OTHER INFORMATION:

- [ ]
- [ ]
- [ ]
- [ ]
- [ ]

RETURN TO SHIP BY:

ALL ABOARD!

PRE-CRUISE TO DO LIST & CHECKLIST

1 MONTH BEFORE	2 WEEKS BEFORE
1 WEEK BEFORE	2 DAYS BEFORE
24 HOURS BEFORE	DAY OF TRAVEL

CRUISE PLANNER

WEEK OF:

MONDAY	TUESDAY	WEDNESDAY	THURSDAY
TO DO	TO DO	TO DO	TO DO
MEALS	MEALS	MEALS	MEALS

FRIDAY	SATURDAY	SUNDAY	NOTES
TO DO	TO DO	TO DO	
MEALS	MEALS	MEALS	MEALS

CRUISE PLANNER

WEEK OF:

MONDAY	TUESDAY	WEDNESDAY	THURSDAY
TO DO	TO DO	TO DO	TO DO
MEALS	MEALS	MEALS	MEALS

FRIDAY	SATURDAY	SUNDAY	NOTES
TO DO	TO DO	TO DO	
MEALS	MEALS	MEALS	MEALS

CRUISING TO DO LIST

CRUISE BUCKET LIST

PLACES I WANT TO VISIT:

THINGS I WANT TO SEE:

TOP 3 DESTINATIONS:

CRUISE ITINERARY

Monday

Tuesday

Wednesday

Thursday

Friday

Saturday

Sunday

CRUISE ITINERARY

Monday

Tuesday

Wednesday

Thursday

Friday

Saturday

Sunday

CRUISE ITINERARY

Monday

Tuesday

Wednesday

Thursday

Friday

Saturday

Sunday

CRUISE OVERVIEW

MONTH:

MONDAY	TUESDAY	WEDNESDAY	THURSDAY	FRIDAY	SATURDAY	SUNDAY

CRUISE ACTIVITIES

WEEKLY ACTIVITY TRACKER: M T W T F S S

DAILY ACTIVITY PLANNER

DAILY ITINERARY

ACTIVITY:
TIME:
LOCATION:
WEATHER:

MEAL PLANNER

DAILY EXPENSES

TOTAL COST:

TOP ACTIVITIES

TIME: SCHEDULE:

NOTES:

DAILY ACTIVITY PLANNER

DAILY ITINERARY

ACTIVITY: _____
TIME: _____
LOCATION: _____
WEATHER: ☀️ 🌤️ 🌦️ ☁️ ⛈️

MEAL PLANNER

DAILY EXPENSES

TOTAL COST: [ ]

TOP ACTIVITIES

TIME: | SCHEDULE:

NOTES:

DAILY ACTIVITY PLANNER

DAILY ITINERARY

ACTIVITY: _____
TIME: _____
LOCATION: _____
WEATHER: ☀️ ⛅ 🌦️ ☁️ ⛈️

MEAL PLANNER

DAILY EXPENSES

TOTAL COST: [_____]

TOP ACTIVITIES

TIME: SCHEDULE:

NOTES:

DAILY ACTIVITY PLANNER

DAILY ITINERARY

ACTIVITY: _____

TIME: _____

LOCATION: _____

WEATHER: ☀️ ⛅ 🌦️ ☁️ ⛈️

MEAL PLANNER

DAILY EXPENSES

TOTAL COST: [ ]

TOP ACTIVITIES

TIME: | SCHEDULE:

NOTES:

DAILY ACTIVITY PLANNER

DAILY ITINERARY

ACTIVITY: _____
TIME: _____
LOCATION: _____
WEATHER: ☀️ ⛅ 🌦️ ☁️ ⛈️

MEAL PLANNER

DAILY EXPENSES

_____ _____
_____ _____
_____ _____
_____ _____

TOTAL COST: [_____]

TOP ACTIVITIES

TIME:	SCHEDULE:

NOTES:

DAILY ACTIVITY PLANNER

DAILY ITINERARY

ACTIVITY:
TIME:
LOCATION:
WEATHER:

MEAL PLANNER

DAILY EXPENSES

TOTAL COST:

TOP ACTIVITIES

TIME:	SCHEDULE:

NOTES:

DAILY ACTIVITY PLANNER

DAILY ITINERARY

ACTIVITY: _____
TIME: _____
LOCATION: _____
WEATHER: ☀️ ⛅ 🌦️ ☁️ ⛈️

MEAL PLANNER

DAILY EXPENSES

_____ _____
_____ _____
_____ _____
_____ _____

TOTAL COST: [   ]

TOP ACTIVITIES

TIME:	SCHEDULE:

NOTES:

DAILY ACTIVITY PLANNER

DAILY ITINERARY

ACTIVITY: _____
TIME: _____
LOCATION: _____
WEATHER: ☀️ ⛅ 🌦️ ☁️ ⛈️

MEAL PLANNER

DAILY EXPENSES

TOTAL COST: [_____]

TOP ACTIVITIES

TIME: | SCHEDULE:

NOTES:

DAILY ACTIVITY PLANNER

DAILY ITINERARY

ACTIVITY: _____
TIME: _____
LOCATION: _____
WEATHER: ☀️ 🌤️ 🌦️ ☁️ ⛈️

MEAL PLANNER

DAILY EXPENSES

TOTAL COST: _____

TOP ACTIVITIES

TIME:	SCHEDULE:

NOTES:

DAILY ACTIVITY PLANNER

DAILY ITINERARY

ACTIVITY: _____

TIME: _____

LOCATION: _____

WEATHER: ☀️ ⛅ 🌦️ ☁️ ⛈️

MEAL PLANNER

DAILY EXPENSES

TOTAL COST: [ ]

TOP ACTIVITIES

TIME:	SCHEDULE:

NOTES:

DAILY ACTIVITY PLANNER

DAILY ITINERARY

ACTIVITY:
TIME:
LOCATION:
WEATHER: ☀️ ⛅ 🌦️ ☁️ ⛈️

MEAL PLANNER

DAILY EXPENSES

TOTAL COST:

TOP ACTIVITIES

TIME: SCHEDULE:

NOTES:

DAILY ACTIVITY PLANNER

DAILY ITINERARY

ACTIVITY: _____
TIME: _____
LOCATION: _____
WEATHER: ☀️ ⛅ 🌦️ ☁️ ⛈️

MEAL PLANNER

DAILY EXPENSES

TOTAL COST: [_____]

TOP ACTIVITIES

TIME: | SCHEDULE:

NOTES:

CRUISE FRIENDS

FRIENDS ARE FOREVER

NAME:

PHONE NUMBER:

ADDRESS:

CABIN #:

FRIENDS ARE FOREVER

NAME:

PHONE NUMBER:

ADDRESS:

CABIN #:

FRIENDS ARE FOREVER

NAME:

PHONE NUMBER:

ADDRESS:

CABIN #:

FRIENDS ARE FOREVER

NAME:

PHONE NUMBER:

ADDRESS:

CABIN #:

There's Nothing Like Cruising Life!

CRUISE FRIENDS

FRIENDS ARE FOREVER

NAME:

PHONE NUMBER:

ADDRESS:

CABIN #:

FRIENDS ARE FOREVER

NAME:

PHONE NUMBER:

ADDRESS:

CABIN #:

FRIENDS ARE FOREVER

NAME:

PHONE NUMBER:

ADDRESS:

CABIN #:

FRIENDS ARE FOREVER

NAME:

PHONE NUMBER:

ADDRESS:

CABIN #:

There's Nothing Like Cruising Life!

CRUISE FRIENDS

FRIENDS ARE FOREVER

NAME:

PHONE NUMBER:

ADDRESS:

CABIN #:

FRIENDS ARE FOREVER

NAME:

PHONE NUMBER:

ADDRESS:

CABIN #:

FRIENDS ARE FOREVER

NAME:

PHONE NUMBER:

ADDRESS:

CABIN #:

FRIENDS ARE FOREVER

NAME:

PHONE NUMBER:

ADDRESS:

CABIN #:

There's Nothing Like Cruising Life!

CRUISE FRIENDS

FRIENDS ARE FOREVER

NAME:

PHONE NUMBER:

ADDRESS:

CABIN #:

FRIENDS ARE FOREVER

NAME:

PHONE NUMBER:

ADDRESS:

CABIN #:

FRIENDS ARE FOREVER

NAME:

PHONE NUMBER:

ADDRESS:

CABIN #:

FRIENDS ARE FOREVER

NAME:

PHONE NUMBER:

ADDRESS:

CABIN #:

There's Nothing Like Cruising Life!

MY CRUISE AGENDA

MY CRUISE JOURNAL

DATE:

What I Did Today:

Highlight of the Day:

Thoughts & Reflections:

MY CRUISE JOURNAL

DATE:

What I Did Today:

Highlight of the Day:

Thoughts & Reflections:

MY CRUISE JOURNAL

DATE:

What I Did Today:

Highlight of the Day:

Thoughts & Reflections:

MY CRUISE JOURNAL

DATE:

What I Did Today:

Highlight of the Day:

Thoughts & Reflections:

MY CRUISE JOURNAL

DATE:

What I Did Today:

Highlight of the Day:

Thoughts & Reflections:

MY CRUISE JOURNAL

DATE:

What I Did Today:

Highlight of the Day:

Thoughts & Reflections:

MY CRUISE JOURNAL

DATE:

What I Did Today:

Highlight of the Day:

Thoughts & Reflections:

MY CRUISE JOURNAL

DATE:

What I Did Today:

Highlight of the Day:

Thoughts & Reflections:

MY CRUISE JOURNAL

DATE:

What I Did Today:

Highlight of the Day:

Thoughts & Reflections:

MY CRUISE JOURNAL

DATE:

What I Did Today:

Highlight of the Day:

Thoughts & Reflections:

MY CRUISE JOURNAL

DATE:

What I Did Today:

Highlight of the Day:

Thoughts & Reflections:

MY CRUISE JOURNAL

DATE:

What I Did Today:

Highlight of the Day:

Thoughts & Reflections:

MY CRUISE JOURNAL

DATE:

What I Did Today:

Highlight of the Day:

Thoughts & Reflections:

MY CRUISE JOURNAL

DATE:

What I Did Today:

Highlight of the Day:

Thoughts & Reflections:

Made in the USA
Middletown, DE
29 June 2023

34211992R00084